The Untold

Nadine Burgers

BookLeaf Publishing
India | USA | UK

Presentation by *BookLeaf Publishing*

Web: www.bookleafpub.com

E-mail: info@bookleafpub.com

ISBN : 9789357447119

First edition 2021

DEDICATION

My loves Addisyn and Parker,

your smiles

your hopes

your endless dreams

make me believe

in infinite possibilities

I hope that one day

you will see

all the ways you have

inspired me

you fuel the fire in my soul

always and forever

PREFACE

I realized I lost all ability to feel
but now I am trying to heal

The untold is words written in sentences that
describe the emotions and thoughts of going
through and healing from past horrors.

Some moments should be remembered as words
on a page. To feel what was once felt. To read
what was once written. To remember a memory
that was once lived.

Please

You said you'd love me
like never before
wait, why are you so mad?
have I done something bad?

You didn't mean to, you're sorry.. I know
Just please: stay, don't go
we'll figure it out, i'll never do it again

Count.
To.
Ten.

I'm sorry I didn't clean up that mess
I'm so tired and under a lot of stress
Please, STOP.. You're hurting me
You are right, I'm sorry it's my fault. I agree

I know you love us and you feel bad
but why do you always get so mad
You're hurting and scaring the children and I
wait.. what do you mean you wish you would
die?

I'm sorry, we love you. please, don't take your
own life

Ofcourse I wanted to be your wife
But the kids and I can't continue to live like
this
Stop, NO .. I don't want a kiss

STOP IT, DON'T TOUCH ME, you just got
upset
And now you seem to live without any regret
please don't hit me the kids can see
please.. I beg of you, listen to my plea

someone, please just give us a hand
help me to understand
what changes do I have to make
I know, I've made a lot of mistakes

But it can't be all my fault
I can't be the reason for every assault
But I'm unsure of what I've done
I've started to wish he would just be gone

I want to leave, but when and where
Help me out, please, I am in despair
there seems to be no one who will listen
to a mother in need in my position

I wish it was as easy as 'leave, just get out'
but nobody seems to understand the mind full of
doubt

was it perhaps all my fault, did I provoke him or
will others believe me?
and if they do, to what degree?

people: please stop judging victims of abuse
and use their own behaviour as an excuse
instead believe what they say
it will be the only way
to stop the cycle of domestic abuse

being

My roots may have grown from pain
but my trunk will grow from love
into leaves and flowers
so bright and green
reaching for the sun.

Holding my own in the storm
trusting my strength to not let go
putting my faith in my foundation
to carry through all that life offers.

I may stand strong & alone
Many will come and go
they take parts of me
they leave parts of them
but at the end

I stand Strong
I grow Higher
I carry Myself
I trust my foundation

I AM

strong

Pull my leaves out
break my branches
carf your name &
hit me with sticks

use me are your
hiding spot
sit in my shadow
build a treehouse &
put on a swing

I will continue
to grow
towards the sun
sing my song
in the wind
feel the tears
from the sky

hear my creaks
but don't mistake that
for being weak
hide from the storm
right under me
i'll be the entry
to your fantasy

I will stand
strong and tall
I can break
but I will not fall
you gave me scars
but they will fade

because
I will be home
to a thousand birds
and the sun
will continue
to shine its light
the raindrops
will cleanse my mind
and the wind
will blow away
the pain

so break me and cut me
and use me as you please
but I will never ever
fall to my knees

where

the sun fades
absorbed
by the ocean
tears fill my lips
with unspoken words
eyes
once filled with hope
are dark
like the night sky
without stars
empty and lost
like the leaf
of a tree
in autumn

fallen and forgotten
like the silence
in the crowd
the spoken words
are muted
like the screams
at the bodem
of the ocean

lost and alone

like a feather in the wind
will I soar over mountains
fly where the wind may lead
and land where I am needed

rooting

A flower grows during heavy storms
A tree stands tall in the strongest winds
The sea will move with the strongest current

your heart may be heavy
your body filled with pain
your soul feels empty
but your roots
your core
it is still there

Underneath it all through your toughest battles
you remain

you may not see it
you may not feel it
you may not believe it

but your roots
that what makes you
Strong, fierce & amazing
are still there and they will regrow
into perfect beauty

solitude

hidden
in the silence
of the night

forgotten
by the twinkle
of the stars

buried
deep within
the ocean's blue

the soul
wanders
in solitude

blame

I have been blamed
for other people's actions
I felt so ashamed
when they had that reaction

no explanations
no hesitations
wrong interpretations
based on generalizations

'you put yourself in those situations'

name shaming
victim blaming
vigorously restraining
just for evading

responsibility.

never believed
negatively perceived
I must have misconceived

I should be relieved
that I received

an apology.

alone

alone with
the pain
and
the fear

what if

one day
he will
re-appear

who will be there
to save me then
if it happens
all over again?

secrets

hands touching me everywhere
so young and utterly unaware
taking off my little white underwear
still a baby, not even pubic hair
unable to say NO, it was a nightmare
You told me it was normal, that you care.

One night you loved me, the next day you'd
shout
Never fully understood, there was so much
doubt
Why did you want me, then throw me away
Until it happened again the next day
I didn't know but to do as you say
Nobody knew that I was your prey

But you promised me it was okay

sunkissed

a seed in soil
with roots so deep
will find its way
to be kissed by the sun

ashes

you've set me on fire
called me a liar
try to take away my desire
to fly higher

but

I will rise
like a phoenix
from the ashes

perfect

your eyes
twinkle
like a million stars

your tears
fill the oceans
for the perfect sunsets

your pain
obscures
the sun by the moon

your smile
lights up the world
on a cold sunday morning

your being
is as magical
as the quietest
of nights

you as a whole
is as beautiful
as the rainbow
in the night sky

dream

let's fly above the sun
and swim beneath the sea

sleep on the clouds
and shower under rainbows

sing the song of the rain
and dance alongside the wind

plant the seeds of happiness

become

come and take a walk with me
follow me to the moon
let the storms inspire you
there is so much you can do

come and take a sail with me
and ride out all the waves
let the ocean care for you
wash away your tears

come and fly with me
all the way to the clouds
let the wind set you free
become who you want to be

rose

a rose is loved for being a rose
with flaws
and imperfections
thorns to protect
each petal unique
together as a beautiful whole

you are loved for being you
your scars, flaws
and imperfections
your strengths, dreams
and unique trades
together as a whole

lovely, beautiful and perfect
in your imperfections

a rose does not compare itself
to another rose
a rose is not less of a rose
by not being loved as a rose

a rose is a rose
and you will always
be you

secrets

for years there was silence
believing it was a choice
wishing it would never be
anything more than a bad memory
but the heavy weight of the consequence
that was inflicted by your lose hands

always kept my mouth shut
for no-one would've believed me

your twisted mind
got me to believe
it was love
now I finally see
the burden you put on me
while you live consequence free

luckily I can finally see
so clearly what's in front of me
why I accept the things I accept

I can grow towards the light
keep you far out of sight
leave all the darkness behind

you can keep that piece you took from me

it will only be part of our secret history

golden

as the night falls
and the sun sets
the whispers fade
in the darkness

the shining
of the brightest stars
swallow the torment
of the days left behind

that moment of silence
fills your existence
with the warmth
of the golden sun

as the moment passes
and the numbing sets in
remember
your fire is within

exist

as my soul wanders
from heaven to hell
depleted by the scars
of all that is forgotten
fueled by the contemplation
of what once was
will never be

all that is left
is existing

warmth

you should never have to say
I have survived another day

You should never have to cry
until your tears are dry

You should never have to wonder
for the next time there might be thunder

you should never have to be afraid
because your safety has been betrayed

there is no easy way
just to get away
but one day
maybe even far away
there will be better days

a day where your tears
might not dry crying
and the rays of the sun
will touch you

like a peck on the cheek
Soft, tender & warm

and the fear
will melt away
like ice
on a sunny day

promise

a gentle soul
a heart of gold
soft-spoken
but broken

I wish I could dissolve your pain
with sunshine and a little rain
with rainbows and flowers
showing you, your superpowers

But your broken heart
it tears you apart

your smile
once so warm
feels cold
like the rain

I am sorry
I could not take you away
to a perfect little bay
just you and me
peaceful for infinity

I promise you today
there will be better days

and we will fly
to a perfect rainbow sky

inspiration

I am letting go
of expectations
changing the narrative
of the conversation

I have no obligation
in the preservation
of this situation

I have to become
my own salvation
for my personal
transformation

I don't owe
any explanations
for my motivations

my imagination
doesn't need
justification
it is my
inspiration